The 15 Laws of Failure
Is What You Are Doing Now Really Working?

BE HONEST WITH YOURSELF

Copyright

Disclaimer

This publication is intended to provide helpful and informative material. It is not intended to diagnose, treat, cure, or prevent any health problem or condition, nor is intended to replace the advice of a physician. No action should be taken solely on the contents of this book. Always consult your physician or qualified health-care professional on any matters regarding your health and before adopting any suggestions in this book or drawing inferences from it.

The author and publisher specifically disclaim all responsibility for any liability, loss or risk, personal or otherwise, which is incurred as a consequence, directly or indirectly, from the use or application of any contents of this book.

Any and all product names referenced within this book are the trademarks of their respective owners. None of these owners have sponsored, authorized, endorsed, or approved this book.

Always read all information provided by the manufacturers' product labels before using their products. The author and publisher are not responsible for claims made by manufacturers.

Paperback Edition

Manufactured in the United States of America

Table of Contents

About The Author

Michael Wolfe currently works in the health and wellness industry and has been both in personal practice in clinic and in sport for over 25 years. During this time he has interacted with people from all walks of life and industry. People find him to be trustworthy and a good listener. He has discovered many parallels in developing youth in sport with challenges faced by both employee and employer. Communication and a positive influence go a long way to helping people heal from injury. This carries over to the business environment in which people face difficult situations.

Michael has always taken a keen interest in human behavior and has developed a passion for helping people work towards their true potential in their chosen field. He is a self-proclaimed good listener and adviser with the ability to see things from different perspectives.

It is through in depth conversations, observations and personal experience that this book was born.

Introduction - Why the 15 Laws of Failure

The 15 laws of failure takes a look at life from a different perspective. These are observations from life of thoughts and behaviours that have lead people to fail. The choices of your thoughts and behaviours have brought you to where you are today. Are you reaching your potential personally and professionally or are you running everything into the ground?

In many ways personal and business failure are very much entwined with one another. As you go through this book ask yourself if you can identify with any of the situations presented from either a personal or professional level.

Chances are you will know someone who lives their life in some of the ways mentioned in this book. Scary thought: maybe after reading a chapter or two or even the entire book you may feel as though you are looking at the reflection of yourself in the mirror.

This is a book based on observations and personal experiences. I hope you can see the benefits in this book so that in turn you can become successful or take yourself to that next level.

In this book you will be introduced to different laws that are not in the mainstream. Most likely you have heard of the *Secret, The Law of Attraction and The Law of Success*.

The law of failure and its new laws offer another perspective on life. This book will give you a different way of looking at things.

Think about it for a second, if we do not live on the edge, the world becomes a crowded space. Is that the world you want to live in?

My sole purpose for writing this book is to give you a different perspective on life to help you make the decisions you need to move your life forward, if you choose to do so.

Here's to your future success.

Michael Wolfe

Chapter 1: The Law of "Soloism"

Yes the law of soloism does not exist in pop culture. It is a term that I have created. Simply put, the law of soloism is doing everything on your own without the help or guidance of a coach, mentor, friend, or family member. In other words you do everything by yourself. This is the lone wolf syndrome...

You must be so intelligent, bright, smart and sophisticated that you do not need the help of others to move ahead in life. If this is your personal choice I wish you the best of luck. This is a road for failure. Ask yourself how many people or businesses became successful by doing it on their own. I challenge you to seek this out and prove me wrong.

I would like to share with you three different examples in which doing your own thing leads to failure.

The first example is from sport. Let us look specifically at individual sports. In particular let's look at one of the most popular individual sports, golf.

Take for example a successful professional golfer. They need a golf coach, a strength and conditioning specialist, a therapist and they need an agent to market them. Can they do this on their own? The answer is no.

These people for the golfers form a team which would be considered a "mastermind group".

The second example is personal. In my first year at University I thought I was better than the information that was taught. I'll never forget getting back my first research paper – 45%. Major Fail! It was worth close to 20% percent of my final mark. My mark now leading to finals was 55%. I needed to reach at least 85% on the final exam to pass the course with 65% or I would fail out of physical education. I was scared. I decided to spend some time with a couple of the brighter students who taught me how to study for the course. I did not want to fail and feel the embarrassment. I worked very hard, pulled an all-nighter and passed the final exam with an 87%. I just passed the course with a 65%. Had I tried to study solo I know I would have definitely failed.

On the bright side I looked for help for my research writing and I was blessed to have an awesome tutor. After spending four sessions with her I was able to grasp the formatting and technique for writing research papers. My marks on any future research paper were never less than 85%. After that experience in first term of first year university I always made sure that I was in a study group.

Participating in a study group was essential for me to pass as each person in the group had a different positive effect on the outcome of studies.

The last example I would like to give you comes from business. I want you to ask yourself if you know of any successful big business that is run by one individual - one individual who has the vision, who can do the grunt work, who can do the marketing, who can do the finances, the technical work, and build relationships; that is one person who can do it all?

Chances are you will not be able to find such a business. Most successful businesses have a corporate structure in which there is a CEO, CFO, COO, President and a few vice presidents of different divisions. This group of people make an executive team. Collectively this group leads the company. The CEO is the visionary, the CFO takes care of the bottom line and the COO is responsible for day to day activities along with the VP's.

The idea here is that you have to have a mastermind group. Most successful people or businesses form a mastermind group whether they realize it or not.

If we look at the example from school, this could be a study group or a tutor. This also applies to the sole proprietor and small business owner. To me it's all the same. There are opportunities to share ideas and give support. No one person should be an island unto themselves if they want to succeed personally and professionally.

Today's technology provides you with the tools to form your own mastermind group on the internet.

There are groups on both linkedin.com and facebook.com for you to join. Finally, take a look in the mirror and ask yourself do I need a mentor, coach or a mastermind group to move forward in my life.

Chapter 2: The Law of Blindness

The law of blindness refers to an individual or business going through life without a chief aim, goal or target. If you or a business want to get somewhere it is important to have a chief aim and a plan to get there. People and businesses fail if they do not know where they want to go. Perhaps some people are just happy with the status quo. Are you?

Have you ever wondered why horses wear "blinkers" for their eyes? It is thought that by wearing the blinkers the horse can stay focused on what is ahead of him / her rather than being distracted by everything else in their presence. Whether or not it is effective is another story; however it gives the horse a focus to look ahead.

Do you have a chief aim? Does your business have a chief aim? If so what is it and what is the plan for you to get there?

If we go back to the example of the golfer the chief aim is to win every golf tournament. To get there he or she needs to have a good long drive and accurate putting skills. He/she needs to build a team around them to help execute this chief aim. Without this team they would fail! This team is the mastermind as referred to in the previous chapter.

In a team setting the object is to win every game played. What sets apart a winning team from a losing team? Of course there are many factors such as skill, experience and work ethic. That being said most winning teams have a definite chief aim. In this case it would be the strategies and tactics set out by the coach and implemented by the players. If we break this down further each individual player is given a role to play with their own chief objective or goal to accomplish in the game. Collectively this is how a team wins because each player's goal or objective blends in with the chief aim of the team. Most of the time this leads to victory.

Teams that fail lack an identity. These teams may have winning as their chief aim; however each individual lacks a specific role or does not play to their "potential".

In your personal life do you live on a day to day basis where you get up in the morning, take a shower, have breakfast, drive into work or take the transit, do your job as needed, come home, watch TV, go to sleep and repeat this cycle? If this is all you want to do and you are happy with that then that is your choice. However if you aspire to do more and receive more then you need to have a chief aim or objective and put a plan in place to get you where you need to go. Perhaps you need a life purpose...

We are blind in life if we do not have a chief aim. . What were you put on this earth to do?

Even though events i.e. natural disaster, sickness may result in temporary failure, the business that has a chief aim and focus will overcome this obstacle and in time will be successful.

If you think about it, a business is created to solve a problem or problems in life in exchange for money. The greater the demand there is to solve a problem, the greater the opportunity to serve both publicly and privately. I'm sure you are already familiar with that saying; however, this is a good reminder. Ask yourself do you or your business solve a problem?

If we look at an insurance company, it is set up to provide coverage for both individuals and businesses. Within that company they have divisions that specialize in home, auto, and commercial insurance. Each department has a specific aim to provide the best coverage possible. The owner has the chief aim or vision to grow the business while the department heads of each division have the mandate aim of providing quality service, retention and growth. If there is no chief aim within each department the vision of the company fails or is rarely met. This can and will lead to bankruptcy.

Each step here leads to a greater possibility of being successful on a daily basis. Having a chief aim supported by a mastermind group is a step towards success and movement away from failure.

Chapter 3: The Law of Self Doubt

"I don't think I can do it, I can't do it, do you think I can do it?" Have these thoughts ever entered your mind? If they have this is the law of self-doubt. What is the law of self-doubt? The law of self-doubt is being negative and not believing in yourself. Failure is inevitable with this type of attitude. You could even call it a negative self-fulfilling prophecy.

This occurs at any age. The other day I witnessed this first hand at soccer training. A young boy was off to the side of the field with his head down. I asked the coaches if they knew why he was over there and one of them thought it was because he was embarrassed because he could not perform the drill that was demonstrated. So I went over and asked him what he was doing. The first words out of his mouth were "I can't do it". I then asked him to give it a try and said I would help him. "I tried and I can't do it" was his response. I spent a few more minutes with him until he got up and gave it another attempt. This broke my heart to see a seven year old child with such strong negative emotions.

Where did that come from? Why didn't he ask for help? Was there support at school? The point here is that this negative mindset can start at an early age. How many negative people do you know who are successful both personally and professionally?

***if you are a teacher, coach, person in authority at work it is important to keep in mind the words you use:

OLD SCHOOL "that's crap, you're stupid, and you don't know how to do anything"

NEW SCHOOL **"how can you improve, how can I help, what if we look at it differently, yes you can"*****

Sometimes your confidence is undermined because of the authority figure you work under or specific people or a specific person in your mastermind group tends to be negative all the time. Unfortunately these people refuse to look in the mirror or take responsibility for their own actions. I know this first hand as I have been that person and have worked with that type of person. It is important to recognize this and to keep their comments in perspective.

Perhaps the most challenging place to be is within a relationship. Take a look around you and ask yourself "am I in a positive environment?" This could be a partner, family or even work. If you are that is great! If you are not then you need to find someone or go somewhere where the environment is positive... I know easier said than done.

You can also form your own mastermind group of likeminded people.

With the 7 year old boy the extra time I spent with him he was able to see himself be successful in his ability to do the soccer drills. He was able to improve to improve his ability and left with a smile on his face.

Amazing what a few minutes can do!

Next you need to be aware of "dream stealers" or "energy sucking vampires."

The Dream Stealer or Energy Sucking Vampire

In life we all come across this person in one form or another. They could be your best friend, husband, wife, partner, brother, sister, father, mother, co-worker. This person takes many forms. They all have one thing in common. They criticize you for what you do because they do not possess the strength that you do to move forward.

The dream stealer may even be in your mastermind group

Unfortunately many of these 'dream stealers' have been unsuccessful in their own attempts and believe because they did not succeed that you will not succeed. Many times these dream stealers act the way they do towards you because they believe the actions or the goals that you have set for yourself may leave you open to criticism and they don't want you to get hurt. Most of the time they do this because they "care" for you.

Dream Stealers put you in a box because they only see you one way. They see what you do and put you in a box. They will praise you when you do something well, something that you are trained to do. However, as soon as you decide it is time to do something else or attempt to do something that you are driven to do or try to do, they have difficulty believing that you will be successful. The dream stealer has difficulty believing that you have the ability to expand your skills and broaden your horizons, especially if it is something unrelated to what you currently do.

Energy Sucking Vampires say things like 'who do you think you are. You know nothing about that? Keep doing what you already know and are good at.' Generally this comes from a place of caring. It also comes from a place of fear of losing you or jealousy. As you change you may find that your relationships change. Such is life.

Dream Stealers could also be the voice of competition afraid of being left in the shadows. They put you down before you even get started. By the time you are up and running they are the ones running to you for help.

Dream Stealers may also be part of your mastermind. They are the people that tell you things don't work when they haven't put in the effort to make things work.

Avoiding the law of self-doubt is a challenge when you have been surrounded by negative talk that has become engrained in your mind. It may take a life time and a lot of help from others to overcome this.

If you have a chief aim and surround yourself with a positive mastermind group you are on the way to overcoming the law of self-doubt.

The mastermind group is a great place to refresh and energize yourself from the negativity that surrounds you. There is strength in numbers when the chief objective of each person is the same. The mastermind group provides support.

The mastermind group also gives a different perspective on issues, a way to look at situations differently. The group as a whole may have one major objective and the people in the group will have a different way of getting there. This is what makes the mastermind so special and helps you get moving in the direction of your chief aim.

Now you have a way to deal with dream stealers or energy sucking vampires. You may want to write a list of three to five people who you can talk to who will help you raise your energy level to a level of confidence.

Chapter 4: The Law of Herd Mentality

Following everyone will get you nowhere fast. Would you rather follow a parade, watch it go by or be the leader. Everyone is different. The law of Herd Mentality relates to being safe. You do whatever other people do. If you do what other people do how does this make you any different and how does it separate you from the pack?

If you are content with the status quo you will stay where you are or you will be left behind.

How many people do you know that are followers who have grown and moved ahead in life? My guess is very few. Fortunately or unfortunately depending on your perspective many people view personal growth as the result of the size of your wallet. In other words what is your bottom line? How much money do you make? What is your net value?

Let's take a look at how this applies in the real world. Look at the structure of a bank. A bank is comparable in some ways to an insurance company in which there are various levels of 'authority' leadership depending on your perspective. It is a pyramid.

A pyramid has many levels and divisions. The lowest level for argument sake is the teller. Next position up is head teller then supervisor then assistant bank manager then branch manager. As you can see this can carry on to district manager to national manager or vice president on to president then COO, CFO and CEO etc.

As you look at the levels there are less people at the higher levels. Each level represents an increase in pay. You will also see a similar type of structure at university, college, sports teams, private business and associations.

Perhaps you are involved in one of these structures? What separates the levels from one another? Are you looking to move up the ladder / pyramid? If so what do you think you need to do to separate yourself from the herd? Or are you comfortable and accepting of your current position or role?

Many times the person who takes **initiative** is the one that leads the herd. So what exactly is initiative? Chances are you probably know; however for the purpose of avoiding failing I will remind you. **Initiative is taking positive action that benefits both you and the people around you without being asked.**

Complaining is not taking initiative. Finding a solution to a problem or a situation you are not happy with is taking initiative.

Taking initiative does a few things to avoid failure. It gets you noticed. It gets the business noticed. It creates a positive environment. It opens the door for you to have more opportunities and people will start to trust you and have confidence in you.

Sometimes initiative is just doing a little extra, doing a little more than what you are paid for. I will talk about this in more detail in *Chapter 8 Being Adequate*.

To avoid failure you need to break away from the crowd. You need to take initiative and risk negative chatter. You need to have confidence in what you are doing. You need to have a chief aim. Ask yourself **"Will the actions I take benefit me, those around me and the business I'm in?"**

In the process of taking initiative it creates a positive impression to those around you. Think about this: when you do something that benefits everyone around you what do you think will happen later if you have a goal or an objective to share with everyone else and you need their support to accomplish this? How likely will they be willing to work with you to achieve this goal? I'm guessing they will...

Showing initiative is just one aspect of leadership. You are setting the example for others to follow. This will separate you from the herd!

Your homework or assignment should you choose... is to look at your job and see what you can do differently without being asked that will benefit you, others and the work you are involved with.

Chapter 5: The Law of Acceptance

Individual failure or lack of success can occur because of lack of thought. It ties in with the herd mentality. Another way of looking at this is through the Law of Acceptance. The Law of Acceptance is an individual's inability to think for themselves and allows others to do the thinking for them. Do you think you can grow and get better by just toeing the status quo?

Have you looked at doing work from a different perspective or changing or modifying your behaviour in different situations?

Do you ever think outside the box? How do you think other businesses separate themselves from the rest?

I'm sure you are familiar with the term "just do it". That is thinking outside the box and I'm fairly confident that most people know that this this slogan was created by Nike.

Sometimes the simple and creative things produced take businesses to a new level of brand recognition. If you live in Canada wouldn't you want to do your banking with a financial institution that tells you that you are "Richer Than You Think.?"

Who do you associate with as the "King of Beers.?"

If you think about it both you and I go about our days and do are our jobs as we are supposed to. What if you could say something different or do your task differently or create an easier way of doing things using your imagination?

Perhaps focusing on this will make you stand out? How can you get yourself noticed above and beyond anyone else you work with?

Remember that within you lies the ability to think outside the box. A unique way to way to get yourself going is to ask yourself at night, before you fall asleep, to find a way to do your work creatively. I know this sounds a bit corny… however why not give it try? You may be surprised at the response you get when you wake up in the morning or in the middle of work the next day.

This where you need to think outside the box. This where you need to harness your imagination.

When I used to teach Anatomy I introduced the "hot seat." This is how it worked: I would have one student volunteer as the body, one student volunteer to do the timing and the rest of the class would be the examiners. I would leave the room and have them put on the board three things for me to find when I came back in. The tables were reversed!

So when I did this I was able to show the students the expectations for their practical exam. This was great for the students because they know knew exactly what they had to do.

Not only that the students were able to be as picky as I was. This "hot seat" was only done in the classes I taught and it separated me from the other instructors. Students gained a new level of respect for me as I put myself out there.

Chapter 6: The Law of Apathy

One of the best ways to fail in life is to be apathetic. This introduces us to the "Law of Low Energy". How many do you interact with that suck the energy right out of you? You know the type of person you need to continually "try" to motivate and in the end you are worse off than when you started?

How many low energy people do you know who are successful in life? Successful people that I meet have a buzz about them. With some people it is subtle and others are in your face. Both you and I know that action speaks louder than words. That being said low energy people show themselves through lack of action or lack of passion.

People who fail do so because they stay as is instead of taking action. Think about this for a second, if you are passionate about something and really enjoy what you do it will show through the actions you take. This does not mean you have to be loud and vocal but you take action with the necessary steps and you do it with a smile on your face.

Here are some signs and symptoms of the Law of Low Energy:

Signs are things people show: look tired, look unhappy, look disinterested

Symptoms are feelings: tired, uninspired, depressed, unhappy, negative, and suicidal

If you recognize any of these signs or symptoms in yourself consider this a warning sign. I say this because I have personally experienced all of them at some point in my life.

To me, low energy, is the most detrimental situation. It literally could be life threatening. **If you believe you fall into this law of low energy please seek help!**

This leads us into the **Law of High Energy.** Have you ever been in room with several people when suddenly there appears to be a change of energy? People stop and take notice. Usually that happens when someone of high energy enters the room and they give off a positive "vibe". People stop because they want to know what's going on. What is this person going to say or do? This person is usually enthusiastic about what they do. They carry a presence or perception of importance.

Have you noticed that with your employer or an employee? You want to be around that person because just being with them gives you a sense of confidence in what you are doing. You can be that person too. This can also happen in a social setting.

Perhaps there was something in the past that got you really excited? Try to remember what it felt like. Go back to that time and place and try to recreate that feeling. How does that make you feel now?

Each morning when you get up and every night when you go to bed relive that situation; feel those same feelings. This is just the beginning. As you continue to do this on a consistent basis there will be subtle changes in your behaviour. The fog that has been over you will soon disappear. Be persistent and keep at it. You will only be the better for it. Yes it does take time and that has been my experience. It is always a challenge when we have to look deep into our soul and spirit.

It is an ongoing process.

Chapter 7 the Law of Recklessness

Are you reckless in your activities? In other words are you doing things without putting thought into what you are doing? Let us look at the definition of recklessness. Recklessness is the state or quality of being or taking unnecessary risks. This leads us to the Law of Imbalance.

Here is an example of what I believe you can relate to. Think about a time when you purchased a new vehicle. You were so excited when you got that new car that as soon as you got it off the dealership floor you decided to take it out for a "spin". Although you knew the speed limit you decided to test out the "performance" of the car anyway. Although you did this before purchasing, you really want to give it your "true" test drive.

So now here you are in a 100km speed zone going 120km/hr. You have to ask yourself is going over the speed limit an unnecessary risk? This limit is put out on the roads to **balance** the speed of drivers in hopes of reducing unnecessary accidents.

If you think about it most car accidents are the results of either speeding or driving too close. This is reckless driving. Have you ever been in a car accident or received a speeding ticket?

The same can be said about the way you spend money or your choice of food for your meals.

Sometimes in business an owner will spend money on the hunch that a lot of money is going to made. That can be a reckless decision if the amount projected is significantly lower than the money that is made. Spending beyond your means is doing the same thing. This can lead to personal bankruptcy.

Both you and I need to learn to work effectively with money to balance our budgets.

Look at some lottery winners who win millions of dollars. Many believe that since they have so much money that there will never ever be a risk of being without. Unfortunately poor money management for some of these people leads them to a financial doom which is worse than where they were before winning the lottery. They decided to spend without serious thought instead of creating a balanced budget. Money is powerful and you can be reckless with it. Do you spend above your means? Be careful because somewhere down the line you may lose perspective of what you have and lose most of it.

This is similar with people and food. Have you ever found something that tastes great and that's all you want to eat? Being reckless with food will lead you to weight gain and predispose you to chronic illnesses like diabetes, heart disease, heart attack and stroke. There are so many diet fads but common sense tells us that eating a balanced "diet" is the best way to maintain optimal health.

I know as I have a sweet tooth.

Another way to look at recklessness is following a philosophy to the extreme. For example, one of the most popular ways to teach is through guided discovery. The idea here is to give students a few guidelines to figure out a problem instead of the teacher, coach or instructor giving a detailed step by step direction.

It becomes reckless and loses its balance when the instructor, teacher or coach goes to the extreme and says "figure it out" without giving some guidance.

You need to have balance so that there is learning for everyone. If you stay quiet and do not ask questions in a guided discovery approach this will lead to a breakdown. Asking questions triggers the mind of the students. This leads to more independent thought and better problem solving abilities for the students in the future.

It is important to find a balance in what you do so as not to be going off the tracks.

You want to be enthusiastic about the work you do; however it is important to know when to curb that enthusiasm as it can be overbearing for some and inappropriate at times.

Take a look at what you are doing on a daily basis. Is there balance in what you do? Is your life balanced between work, friends and health? If not there is a good chance you are doing a lot more of one thing and letting the other two fade away. This increases your chance of failure. Here is a great opportunity to ask for help from your mastermind.

Chapter 8: The Law of Adequacy: Introducing The Min- Max Principle

Have you ever come across someone who says to you that they love what they do so much they would do it for free?

Is that you?

Many people fail in what they do because they expect to receive either praise or monetary reward if they do extra. Just doing enough or little and expecting a lot in return does not work. Let me introduce you to the min –max principle. The min- max principle basically means you do minimal or adequate work and expect to get phenomenal results.

I have witnessed this myself with students who I have taught when they decide only to do the work while in class to prepare for exams and do nothing once class is finished. They believe what they have done in class is adequate to pass. They write their exam and then wonder why they failed. If they had studied outside of the classroom chances are they would have passed.

I have seen this with soccer players who claim they want to play internationally or get a scholarship. They show up for training only and do nothing extra. They only show up for scheduled practices and do not do anything extra to make themselves better at what they do. They expect that by doing the minimum they will get great results

Doing the minimum or doing what is adequate will not get you further ahead. You are staying the status quo or you are fading away.

How do you want to be remembered?

If you are passionate about what you do you will have the ability to do that little extra because you know that it will make a difference somewhere down the line. Sometimes you need to do a little extra without getting paid or getting the recognition. It is habit forming.

People fail because of poor habits. People get recognized because of good habits such as doing a little extra.

Take a look at your life and ask yourself is there something more you can do on a regular basis that will make a positive difference for your environment?

===
***If you are in a position of leadership it is vital that you acknowledge those you lead who do extra work ***

There are a few reasons for this. First it reinforces the value of the work they do. They feel appreciated. As a leader it shows that you recognize the extra work and effort. This is important because many leaders only recognize individuals when things go sour. Next it creates a positive environment to be in.

Failure to acknowledge individuals who put in extra effort can lead to disgruntled employees. It will have employees second guess their self-worth to the company or leadership. Employees will feel that they are unappreciated and taken for granted. Depending on what the employee is doing they may stop doing the extra work and just do what they are paid to do or they will leave.

As an employee it is up to you if you want to do extra. Perhaps it is in your nature that you always do extra. Doing more than what you are paid for may lead to other opportunities either with your current work or somewhere else. Perhaps your extra work catches the eye of another employee who moves up the ladder and then takes you along for the ride.

The opposite of this is someone who puts others down in order to make themselves look good. This is the 'me, myself and I' complex. I will talk about this further in chapter 13.

Chapter 9 The Law of Unpleasant

How many unpleasant people do you know who are very successful? How many negative people do you know who are successful? Ever notice that negative people do not get very far.

Your personality and the way you carry yourself has a direct effect on you and others around you. People will only put up with negativity for so long until they tune it out. I know I've been guilty of that in the past.

Years ago when I was in the camping industry I had been overlooked for a leadership position and returned as councillor with a chip on my shoulder. Although I was pleasant on the outside I was negative about everything that was around me. It left me questioning whether or not I should even be there. I was questioning my self-worth. Other staff members did not want to be around me and my campers did not have the greatest experience. Everyone saw through me.

Just when I thought I would throw in the towel one of the senior staff said to me "Mike you got a raw deal. You should have been the Junior Section Director. Everyone knows it. You've got two choices. Either continue like this or show everyone why you should have had that position." Talk about a wakeup call. Someone recognized my frustrations and was kind enough to acknowledge how I was feeling.

Internally things slowly changed for me after that. Perhaps there was a genuine pleasing personality in me after all...

What I did notice through this change was that I was getting more opportunities to run and create programs. This change in attitude and personality eventually led to recognition from the staff who identified me as the person who embodied the spirit of the camp and earned a prestigious leadership award from the camp director. There were others just as deserving to receive both awards. I was humbled and honoured at the same time. This encouraged me to continue to give extra and be pleasant.

It is possible to go from failure to success if you change from being negative to positive. It is a choice that you make each and every single day. It is also a habit you need to develop. Moving from a place of negativity to a place of positivity is different for everyone. That is why it is so important to be around those who lift you up. (Mastermind group)

One of the ways I changed was that I looked for one good thing I liked about someone and complemented them. I was sincere and I truly believed what I was saying.

The reactions from people were special. Many were surprised and at first thought that I wanted something in return. Even though it may have been something as simple as complimenting their work with their cabin, I could feel the difference it made to them.

It is so easy for you and me to get stuck on being negative when there is so much to be positive about. If we point out the positive it has a ripple effect. This is similar to "paying it forward". Think about it for a second. If I compliment you and the work you have done, what happens to you? Certainly it has a ripple effect!

First, I am going to feel good about your response. Next you will feel good about the compliment. Third you will carry that with you throughout the day and so will I. Finally you may pass this on to someone else.

If you are in a leadership position this is the key to sending positive messages from the top down.

Chapter 10 The Law of Distraction

How many times have you started to do something and stop to answer the phone or read an article on the internet or get caught up in a conversation and then fifteen or twenty minutes later you realize just lost time to get work done? This is no different than an athlete getting caught up in comments shouted by unruly fans. This type of continuous behaviour leads to failure because nothing gets accomplished.

We all have several things that we want to get done. The key here is to pick one thing and focus on the steps necessary to accomplish that goal. I'm sure this is nothing new to you but it is a good reminder.

Laser focus on the task at hand will move you closer to your end goal. It is also possible that as you get closer to that end goal that goal may change. Again the key is to keep it simple. Focus on the things you need to do each day to move yourself forward.

Perhaps you are familiar with this example for focus. Imagine it is a sunny day and you are stranded on an island with only a magnifying glass and you have to get a fire going. What would you do? Obviously you would look for as much wood and kindling as possible. Next you position the magnifying glass so it intensifies the heat from the sun's rays to a specific spot on the wood. Because of the focus of the heat from the sun's rays through the magnifying glass you now have a fire. Laser focus of the heat generated from the sunrays started the fire.

Look at the amount of time you have each day and break it down into 15 -45 minute segments. In each 15 minute chunk of time write down an activity you need to do to move you closer to that ultimate goal.

This is time well spent and you will avoid failure.

At this time I want to introduce to you the **Law of Jack of All Trades and Master of None**

Law of Jack of All Trades and Master of None

Being a jack of all trades may or may not lead to success or failure. A jack of all trades is able to do **many things adequately**. It is similar to multitasking.

Multitasking has a few different meanings

1. It can mean performing two or more tasks simultaneously.
2. It can involve switching back and forth from one thing to another.
3. Multitasking can involve performing a number of tasks in rapid succession.

Research has proven that multitasking is not beneficial to being successful.

Some studies suggest that multitasking can reduce productivity as much as 40% (Rubinstein, Joshua S.; Meyer, David E.; Evans, Jeffrey E. 2001)

Being a master of one suggests that you possess **specialized knowledge** or have a **specialized skill**. This is more valuable than being a jack of all trades. People pay more money for specialized skill. They pay because there is a higher **perceived** value. Does a family physician make more money than an orthopedic surgeon? I doubt it. An orthopedic surgeon has specialized skills compared to a family physician. The orthopaedic surgeon had to do extra schooling to get to that level of expertise.

To focus on one skill day in day out is an ongoing process. Do you ever get to a point where you feel you know everything and your mind starts to wander on to something else? When you get to this point it is time to upgrade your knowledge.

Being a jack of all trades indicates that you have lost your vision and that you want to be everything to everyone. It is as though you want everyone to like you. Here's reality. You will not please everyone. I know, I've been there before.

People with specialized skills are leaders in their industry. People follow them. You get noticed.

If you look at most successful businesses they have a leader whose specialized skill is vision and they surround themselves with people who have specialized skills to carry out their vision.

If you look at individuals and businesses that thrive and succeed on the internet they have specialized knowledge that addresses a specific problem. It is unique, different and gets results for their customers.

The Law of Being Busy – The Make Work Project Syndrome

Along with being the Jack of all trades there is also a tendency you may fall into which is creating work projects just to occupy your time instead of focusing on what you need to do to move yourself or your business forward.

Take for example a successful company that rests on its laurels of previous accomplishments. Look at a company that prides itself on customer service with its manager's main focus on improving the communication skills of the customer service reps. Now a new manager is hired and the most pressing thing for them is to have his or her office redesigned. The manager is so focused on this new unnecessary project that they neglect their role in training and guiding the customer service reps. As a result the quality of customer service is decreased and there is loss of business.

This would not have happened if this new manager had focused on working with the people in his or her department.

I believe both you and I know the difference between busy work and effective work or work that has meaning and impact.

Chapter 11 The Law of Misinformation

One of the best ways to avoid failure in what you do is to get the correct information you need to get the job done. A lot of that has to do with putting yourself in the shoes of the market you serve and find out what it is people want and then deliver it to them. Research, research and more research most of the time guarantees that you have the correct information.

This also applies to what happens in your place of work. In any business there will always be rumours and innuendos about things that go on. The key here is to make sure you get the correct information before you make any quick or rash judgements.

Keep in mind that people say things because they are hurt, frustrated or upset by something that is going on inside of them. Instead of dealing with the issue straight on they start dropping hints and incomplete stories to others who will listen.

Having been in leadership roles over the years I have made a point of confronting things head on. Seek the truth. Most of the time the issues are trivial at best.

Office gossip I believe would be the best way to look at it. People get hurt and lose jobs over false accusations and negative gossip. This ultimately can lead to both personal and business failure.

One of the best places to see that correct information is important is in the trading industry. Now, I do not have any experience in this field. I do know that your most successful stock brokers have done the most thorough research on trends. They take the information they receive and assess for accuracy.

If you look into the realm of sports the organization that drafts the best tends to be more competitive and win more championships because of the player they have identified, and developed.

Scouts send information to management and then decisions are made. One the best examples of an organization that gets the correct information is the Detroit Redwings of the National Hockey League. Two of their best players were ranked very low in the NHL draft; however due to the thorough investigation of the scouting staff they were able to pick these players when other teams passed them over. Pavel Datsyuk was taken 171st overall in the 6th round in the 1998 NHL entry draft and Henrik Zetterberg was picked 210th in the 7th round of the 1999 NHL hockey draft. Both these players were instrumental in helping Detroit win several Stanley Cups in the National Hockey League. This is an excellent example of getting the correct information.

To be successful and avoid failure you need to get the proper information to make educated choices. It is important to do your research and due diligence. Trends and information change over time and you need to know what is current.

In an office situation you need to get specific information from reliable sources about any gossip and allow the specific parties involved to give their points of view. Trust and honesty in this situation is critical.

Chapter 12 The Law of Intolerance

Ever notice that people have habits or ways of doing things that you can't stand? You don't have to look any further than the person you live with or the person you work with. Are you perfect? Sometimes you get caught up in the way or ways you want people to be because it makes it easier for you to deal with them. If you do not tolerate them you let them out of your life.

Sometimes you have to put up with other peoples' baloney. They may have information that will benefit you and others. You must look at the pros and cons of what you are willing to tolerate. It is definitely a personal choice.

As a former teacher, one of the most difficult things to do is put up with the politics of management. The ability to understand that teachers are more easily removed than students is a tough pill to swallow.

The teaching profession today is very different than it was 20-30 years ago. Now students have more rights and the system encourages passing without maintaining standards.

Many teachers must pass students when they deserve to fail. To be successful as a teacher you need to be tolerant to this. Failure is imminent if you don't.

In other organizations and social situations, individuals have different personalities and beliefs. You need to be accepting of this. If you are intolerant it will be difficult for you to move forward.

Religious intolerance is another example. You may have different religious beliefs than someone else.

Have you ever wondered why we have so many wars? Have you ever wondered why it is difficult to have peace in the world? You do not have to look any further than intolerance of other peoples' thoughts, ideas and beliefs.

People get passed by for promotion because they were intolerant to the office politics? They were not willing to play the game. This is a personal choice!

Chapter 13 The Law of Me Myself and I

How many successful people do you know who only think about themselves? Unfortunately many of us who want to do well just think about our own needs. We ignore the needs of others or we make inappropriate comments because we don't understand someone else's situation.

You and I need to look at the bigger picture. If you take action that just helps you then it has no effect on others around you. Sometimes you need to do that. Have you ever thought about the consequences of your actions and the effect positive or negative it has on others?

In a leadership position if you only think about yourself people will pick up on it quickly. You will lose respect and find it difficult to get support and help. As a leader the more people you help get what they want, the more likely you are going to get what you want. "Let me help you get what you want" You can always ask "how may I help you?"

Do you act in ways that focus on what you are doing without any thought as to how it affects others around you? Do you get blinded by selfishness? I've been guilty of this in the past.

Many years ago I was introduced to what I thought was an amazing opportunity in multilevel marketing. I thought I was the most incredible person because I was going to make millions of dollars by getting other people to purchase the products I was using. I was so full of myself that I totally ignored the needs of the people around me.

Enter the "Law of Me Myself and I". You probably know that the most common word we use is I. Think about it for a second. Would you rather hear your name mentioned or someone else's name talked about?

When I thought I was going to build my massive multilevel marketing empire all I could think about was how much money I was going to make. I was thinking about all the material things I could have.

In the process of meeting many people my focus was solely on them buying into what I had to offer. I was oblivious to their needs. Because I was so persistent with what I was doing it cost me some relationships. I burned some bridges and that hurt me personally.

Had I put myself in their shoes, I'm sure my approach would have been different.

I failed miserably at this venture both personally and financially.

This brings to me the next law which has been out there for many years first introduced by Napoleon Hill "Do unto others as you would have others do unto you."

In other words treat people the way you want to be treated. You can also look at it from this view: put yourself in the other person's shoes.

A wise person once said "you were given two ears and one mouth – listen first, speak second. Or also think of it as seek first to understand then be understood. Either way you are putting your needs aside. Remember, as you know, the more people you help get what they want the more you receive in return.

Chapter 14 The Law of Secret Chatter- The Back Stabber

I think you know what this is about. So what exactly is the law of secret chatter? Good question. Let me ask you this. Have you ever been around someone who puts other people down behind their back and are nice to them in person? Is that you? Let's be honest here.

I will admit to have been that person in the past. This usually comes from a place of insecurity and jealousy. My experience has been the back stabber is looking to get ahead of where they are and they think the only way to move forward is to put other people down.

Think about it this way. If you want to move forward and advance people will most likely help you if you have helped them in the past. I do believe there is such a thing as Karma as I have received the short end of the stick in the past because of comments I made.

It is a painful lesson to learn. As someone once said if you cannot say something nice about someone then do not say anything at all. Your silence will speak volumes as compared to speaking your mind.

I believe it is fine to disagree with someone but to personally attack them behind their back will come back to bite you. I've been there and do not wish to be there again.

If this resonates with you, you need to ask yourself why you are saying negative things about other people.

The tougher and more challenging route is to speak with them face to face.

Take a serious look in the mirror and ask yourself "am I a backstabber". Here's the thing, you need to be truly honest with yourself. If you are not, you will not benefit from this message.

I think it is important for you to know that backstabbing and putting people down comes from a place of feeling weak, inadequate or insecure. If you are strong and confident you will deal with whatever is bothering you head on.

That being said instead of backstabbing someone, ask yourself what you can do to make your situation better. If both you and I just focus on what we can control things may or will turn out differently. As it has been said before, it is how you react to a situation and not the situation itself.

Chapter 15 The Law of Family First

The law of family first deals with putting family members in positions of authority or seniority before they have proven themselves. In many small companies a daughter or son or combination of both may take over the business. In businesses in which there are two or three employees or many part time staff this usually works. Problems arise in larger businesses when experienced and visionary employees are overlooked for promotion to management positions that are taken by inexperienced family members. Many times these family members have a sense of entitlement that has yet to be earned.

Several issues arise when these family members are put into these positions. For example they may have an experienced individual with a strong personality under their supervision and would rather avoid working with them instead of showing them they are valued and learn from them. Even the "weakest person" has something to offer a new manager.

Here are a few other things that happen:

1. Resentment towards the company from those who were overlooked.
2. Decrease in loyalty to the company.
3. Loss of trust in the company.
4. Fear of losing one's employment.
5. Low morale.
6. Loss of employees to other companies.
7. Loss of business.

A good example of how to put family members into place was set by Ted Rogers of Rogers Communications. Any of his children that wanted to work at Rogers always started from the bottom so that they would earn the respect of the employees as they worked their way up.

It is quite obvious that business owners need to take a serious look at how they place their children into their business. Unfortunately there are business owners whose sole focus is to have their company run by their children that they are blind to the needs of the business and their executive team that they lose leaders and possibly their business. Is that you?

So if you own a business with wanting your children to take over, I suggest that you have them start from the bottom and work their way up to earn the respect of the other employees. By putting your needs before the business, your business has a good chance of failing. As a business owner it is always good to sit back and reflect as to what is happening in your business and ask your executive team for honest feedback.

You must be able to accept the feedback and move forward with it.

Personal Assessment

Here is an opportunity to review the 15 Laws to discover changes you need to make to take yourself or your business to the next level of growth and development.

1. Are you in a mastermind group?
2. Do you have a chief aim or focus?
3. Do you have confidence and faith in what you are doing?
4. Are you different in what you do or have a unique approach to solving problems? What sets you apart?
5. Do you go with the flow or do things differently
6. Are you energetic about the work you do?
7. Are you balanced in your actions?
8. Do you do more than is expected? Do you show initiative?
9. Are you nice to be around?
10. Are you focused on what you need to do on a daily basis to move yourself or your business forward?
11. Have you done the appropriate research in advance of what you plan to do to get the best results?
12. What is your tolerance level and to what level are you willing to play the game.
13. Are you solely focused on you or do you care about others you work with?
14. Do you keep your negative comments to yourself or do you put other people down to build yourself up?

15. Are you focused on your family instead of what's best for your business?

Answer these questions honestly as they will give you the direction you need to go to move yourself or business forward. In the end the more you help others the more you will succeed!

Final Thoughts

In the end you and I are responsible for the life we want to live. Whether we succeed or not is up to us. You need to decide where you want be. You can choose to fail or choose to succeed.

Whether you say you are a failure or a success, you are correct. It is your choice.

The purpose of this book was to open your eyes to another perspective on life. I am hoping in the process you learned some key valuable things about yourself.

Now you have some ideas as to how to move forward and make changes if you so desire.

As I see it (and this is just one perspective) each day is a great day to wake up with a smile knowing you are moving forward in your life.

Failing at something is one of life's greatest teachers! *You were born to succeed!*

Michael Wolfe

www.ingramcontent.com/pod-product-compliance
Lightning Source LLC
Chambersburg PA
CBHW051244170526
45165CB00004B/1573